THE FORBIDDEN LOVE

A Sixteen Year Old Heart

Arwa Kapadia

BlueRoseONE.com
Stories Matter
New Delhi • London

BLUEROSE PUBLISHERS
India | U.K.

For permissions requests or inquiries regarding this publication, please contact:

BLUEROSE PUBLISHERS
www.BlueRoseONE.com
info@bluerosepublishers.com
+91 8882 898 898
+4407342408967

ISBN: 978-93-7139-755-1

Cover Design: Aman Sharma
Typesetting: Manisha Rawat

First Edition: November 2025

Epigraph

"Two hearts, two voices,
Tied by silence and stray glances.
This is our story–
Told from both sides of the mirror."

Dedication

To those who woke up with deserted eyes, breathing despite swallowing stillness of pain like poison.

The ones who used trembling hands to stitch their hearts and referred to it as healing.

Who offered love with bleeding hands and wielded it like a dagger.

This is for you, the vagrants of invisible wounds and soft wars

Acknowledgment

Thanking to all those, especially my parents who made this possible to publish this literary piece out of all odds.

Note:- *"Each section shifts between perspectives–hers, his, and the quiet space between. The tone of the poems will guide you."*

Her POV- ♥

His POV- ♠

Joint POV- ♦

Author's Note

This is not a diary.

But everything you'll read here
was felt.

Somewhere, somehow.

By someone.

This is not a confession–it's a reflection.

I hope you find your own story somewhere inside mine.

Contents

Section 3-

Section 4-

Section 5-

Prologue

***I wish I had met you in a world
that didn't ask us to choose between love and survival.***

*He walked into my life like a whisper – soft, unexpected –
and left like footprints fading into sand.
I never thought a stranger could feel like someone I was born missing.*

*It started small.
Just a DM.
Just a glance.
Just a few stolen moments in the same room.*

*A presence that felt too familiar, too soon.
I told myself it was just excitement, just the thrill of something new.*

***And truth is – I wasn't some lover girl, floating on fantasies.
I knew what red flags looked like.
I knew the world doesn't always return the love it's given.
But I gave myself a chance anyway.***

A chance to believe.

A chance to try.

A chance to feel something real, even if it never was.

But then, it stayed.

He stayed.

In my thoughts.

In the quiet ache of midnight.

In the noisy rush of daylight.

In the bitter sip of coffee I once shared with him.

In the silence of unsent messages I still draft and delete.

He didn't just stay –

he became a part of me.

He was my every first time.

First thrill.

Bitter sweet cry.

Betrayal.

First taste of loving someone who once knelt down and swore they would never leave.

And what happened between us?

Nothing.

Everything.

Our story didn't break apart loudly like a glass shattering on the floor.

It dissolved – slow, soft, silent – like mist at sunrise.

A sweet evening.
A lingering ache.
A bruise so deep, no hands could ever reach it.

This is our story.
A story stitched together with broken promises and wailing silences.
A story I still live inside, long after he chose to walk away.

Every time this pen meets the paper,
every vein in my body bursts out with blood and pain.

This isn't a confession.
It's a reflection of the wounds that bruised my heart and body,
when I loved someone who once told me I was everything.

Long after he abandoned me,
I was still believing in us.

And here –
this is what remains...

THE BEGINNINGS

"Through the mirror"

♠

The machines howled, the iron roared,
yet through the storm, her spirit soared.
Sharper than blades, her silence screamed,
a living fire I hadn't dreamed.

I tried to speak, *"You've got this too,"*
but fumbled words could not break through.
So I shifted weight, I stood my ground,
hoping she'd hear what stayed unbound.

She lifted weights without a sound,
and in her breath, my heart was found.
I wore my hope like broken skin,
wishing she'd see the war within.

♥

The clang of weights was home to me,
a steady hum, a sacred sea.
But today, a stare broke through the tide,
caught me mid-breath, stripped me wide.

I stumbled once, forgot the count,
his gaze had built a weight I couldn't mount.
A stranger's glance, a shadow's song,
and yet it felt I'd known him long.

Inside the glass, reflections swirled,
a stranger's eyes, my tangled world.
And for a breath, and for a blink,
the gym collapsed; I couldn't think.

♦

No words were passed, no names were called,
just glances flung, just defenses stalled.
In that strange hush, a tether grew,
a thread of gold we never knew.

Quick smiles traced where doubts had been,
a silent vow carved deep within.
Neither moved, neither dared,
yet both stood naked, both stood scared.

A story spun in ghostly thread,
no promises, just things unsaid.
A story lived between two skins,
a war of might-have-beens, begins.

•In A Glance•

♠

Her hair waved like a restless sea,
small hands commanding gravity.
Over dumbbells where empires fall,
she lifted more than just the wall.

Something settled sharp and true,
a feeling fresh, yet strangely due.
When was the last, post gym and sweat,
I didn't picture her – and forget?

A stranger, but stitched into my sky,
her image a scar I can't deny.
She lingers like a worn-out song,
soft and steady, pulling me along.

It was just a glimpse – a stolen view,
but it anchored something I never knew.
Hazel storms, so calm, so deep,
a gaze my restless mind can't keep.

A man too solid for dreams to fake,
etched into thought with every ache.
When he stood there, the air grew thin,
small moment, sharp enough to spin.

When was the last, post clang and hymn,
I didn't see his ghost at the gym?
A stranger, but his silence stays,
brushing my heart in secret ways.

Maybe this ache will melt like rain,
fade into dust, dissolve the strain.
Just a glance, yet it roots too much,
a pull in the spine, a wordless touch.

Like rain falling from unseen skies,
like a promise stitched into lies.
Each drop, a throb, an ancient tune,
two hearts drifting under the same moon.

A fleeting bond — loud, but thin,
a stranger's glance digging in.
Why does it taste like something more,
something fate left at the door?

Lingering Eyes

♥

Mid-rep, I saw a shadow move –
a silent force, too still to prove.
A figure draped in quiet might,
black as dusk, yet full of light.

His hazel eyes – like dusk and dawn –
pulled me in, then wandered on.
I froze, the weight slipped through my palm,
his presence more than threat or calm.

I feared the fall, the fading trace,
yet longed to hold that stolen face.
What was this sway, this silent tide,
that moved within – but couldn't hide?

♠

I saw her eyes through mirrors bent,
like fading stars, soft and intent.
They locked with mine – just for a beat,
then drifted down, unsure, discreet.

She searched for more – or maybe not,
but something stirred, a quiet thought.
Her almond gaze, both warm and wide,
held me still – then stepped aside.

Familiar strangers, souls untold,
aligned in silence, shy and bold.
We can't predict where this will go –
but something waits, and both hearts know.

After four days — how strange, how near,
this ache that blooms with quiet fear.
An invisible thread keeps pulling tight,
day and night, wrong or right.

We don't know what waits down this line,
but time holds secrets, soft and fine.
It slows like breath before a cry,
as if it knows we won't say goodbye.

Familiar strangers, souls untold,
aligned in silence, shy and bold.
We can't predict where this will go —
but something waits, and both hearts know.

Eyes Held

♠

"Hey, you got this," I said,
Words fled like a brook just fed.
She looked away, mid-rep, then back–
Steady focus, no sign of slack.

She's delicate, yet deeply still,
Like bark on a silent hill.
Graceful, quiet, but so composed,
Strength in softness, neatly enclosed.

She lingers, I don't know why–
Like a whisper passing by.
A stranger I've barely seen,
Yet she stays inside each scene.

♥

Yes, please... go ahead," I said – unsure,
my voice too light to feel secure.
He didn't just look, he saw straight through –
and suddenly, I didn't know what to do.

His eyes were dusk, his presence still,
he stood like silence bent to will.
Strong, but unaware of sway,
he stirred the air and stole the day.

It sparked – a glance, a pull, a start,
a candle flickering in my heart.
It felt too quick to name or fight,

Talking felt unreal – like waves we miss,
too quiet to name, too soft to resist.
Four days passed, but they still stay,
echoes we carry in quiet replay.

Butterflies weren't meant to mean much,
but they flare like fire with every touch.
Their hum still lingers in skin and bone –
a closeness we both feel alone.

Something waits – we don't ask why,
just feel the hush as we pass by.
Time may speak what we can't see.
For now, we don't name it. We let it be.

"A Rhythm Shared"

Her smile – warm, unforced, and wide,
lit something quiet deep inside.
It felt like joy I'd long misplaced,
a sudden light I couldn't waste.

I couldn't hide the shift I felt,
a weightless ache, the way I melt.
We passed like ghosts between our sets,
exchanging silence, half-said bets.

"Alternate?" she asked – a breath, a pause,
and time stood still without a cause.
A stranger, yes – but somehow true,
and lifting felt like something new.

♥

Just asking felt like something shy,
but with him, it came out smooth and dry.
His voice – a hush, so calm, so kind,
it quieted the storm inside my mind.

My nerves slipped loose like silk from skin,
his steady grace let softness in.
With every rep, in silent glide,
we moved like waves beneath the tide.

He watched, he smiled, no rush, no race–
just time unfolding, slow and grace.
I left the mat not quite the same –
something had bloomed without a name.

Two hours passed like whispered air,
moments light as an unspoken prayer.
Like butterflies that kissed, then flew,
but left their wings inside us too.

Each glance, each brush, a quiet mess –
so casual, yet weightless stress.
A rhythm bloomed we didn't chase,
too soft for name, too wild for place.

Just one lift, yet something shook,
a breath we shared, a second look.
No words, but somehow we both knew–
a spark had burned, and stayed there too.

Between The Sets

The gym became our quiet ground,
his presence made my fears unbound.
No longer just sweat, just passing days–
but moments I clung to in quiet ways.

He'd smile, he'd stand right by my side,
his words would find what I would hide.
"Go on, one more," he'd softly say –
and fear itself would slip away.

His breath was strained, but still he tried,
each set a battle, pain denied.
And when we'd rest, he'd glance my way –
with eyes that begged for more to stay.

♠

She moved with grace I couldn't name,
like sunlight pouring through the rain.
Stretches, sprints, and then that laugh –
she made each hour cut in half.

Her laughter bloomed between each set,
and brought me back from my regret.
And when her hands began to shake,
I swear time paused for her own sake.

She pushed, she tried – and though I knew,
my weight was double, her will stayed true.
In quiet reps and shared routines,
we left no room for in-betweens.

It's something basic, something deep,
a closeness neither meant to keep.
Unnamed, unclaimed, yet oddly near –
a whisper we both chose to hear.

These glances stay, though never said –
a thread that hums, but isn't led.
Like butterflies that stir the air,
we breathe it in, then leave it there.

Perhaps this line we never tied,
was spun by fate we can't deny.
More than passing, more than now –
as if the stars had made a vow.

SOFT ECHOES

"Stayed In Glances"

♥

So strangely rare, my heart began to ache –
love was never mine to hold or take.
But his dusk-dark gaze caught mine, so still,
a memory that bent to a softer will.

Our fingers brushed – not planned, just fate's old thread.
My skin lit up like fire someone once said.
I told myself that moment wouldn't last,
just charm once seen in stained-glass past.

I said it meant nothing – my pulse knew more.
Why do mirrors echo what we ignore?
His stare stayed longer than it ever should,
and rewound a memory I misunderstood.

♠

A charm that lingers inside my dreams,
a stranger I still see in moonlit gleams.
Waving hair, small hands, soft grace –
her silhouette lives in my quietest space.

I still recall her fingers near mine,
a brush so brief, yet aged like wine.
Her presence pulls in ways I hide,
but I let the feeling drift and slide.

I tell myself this will all erase,
but her image still haunts night's face.
Our eyes once met through mirrored haze –
and that one look, my heart still plays.

No words were shared, but something stayed,
between our glances, a silence laid.
And when we left, it followed us home –
this almost-love we let quietly roam.

We caught each look and still we stared,
but none of us moved, none of us dared.
We lingered too long in that soft song,
a moment that felt like we both belonged.

Brushed hands, a glance – then pulling back,
in this wondering, who takes the track?

The ifs and whys might make us shake,
but the thrill of love still keeps us awake.

"A Second Too Long"

♠

Her beauty and grace are what keep me awake,
my breath grows heavy with each rise she takes.
Her presence drifts by – a gentle, quiet trace,
each step she takes makes my heart race.

Her silence rings loud in the gym's wild throng,
I catch her reflection – we've been watching all along.
She lifts like poetry, calm and strong,
our eyes meet – it feels off, but holds too long.

I swore not to fall again, not now,
but her charm keeps breaking that silent vow.
I try to let go, but she stays too near –
her face carved into thought, vivid and clear.

I don't fall easily, I don't fall with ease.
But near his, my armor feels less complete.
Not in words, not in charms or gaze-
Just in how I soften trough ordinary days.

When he walks by, that ache returns,
A feeling slow, but one that burns.
I lift, I move, I breathe just fine,
Yet somehow, his warmth slips into mine.

I tell myself it's just the way he stands,
just the echo of him brushing my hand.
Still, I sense something I can't quite face –
like I've met this longing in another place.

Unseen but present, a thread took shape,
between the clang of iron and air's escape.
Not through words or fleeting eyes,
but in silences we couldn't disguise.

It wasn't quiet – not fully still –
but questions lingering against our will.
Two strangers circling the same refrain,
both afraid, yet neither in pain.

Something unspoken began to grow,
a weight that stayed, refusing to go.
Not love, not yet – but the start of a choice,
a hush that waits, already with voice.

And somewhere between what we meant and what we hide,
we both knew the change had already arrived.

A Cup Shared Between Us

♠

I see her lift across the mirror maze,
So many days in a row, yet no words exchanged.
We caught each other's glance – a quiet spear through,
Time paused again as a smile slipped through.

Messy hair, sunlight tracing her neck,
Gathering my nerves, I took the step.
"It was a heavy workout... how about a coffee?"
The words escaped, trembling softly.

A graceful nod, a too-sweet "sure,"
As she packed her bag – I knew no cure.
Time stilled, breath shook, glances stole,
And I drowned in the beauty her laughter told.

♥

After days of silence and stolen glances,
A coffee offer – how could I deny such chances?
His shaky tone as he spoke to me,
Matched my racing pulse, perfectly.

My favourite – iced frappe – how would he even know?
"Well made for each other," I joked in flow.
After all, what's in this world for you,
When you came with nothing – how can you go with one too?

No one tracked the hours we spent,
As the sunset whispered where the daylight went.
Lost in talk, in his listening eyes,
My heart raced fast, cheeks warm, no disguise.

♦

It was surreal, so ethereal,
Words dissolved in the evening's mural.
Almost-hands crossed, almost-love near,
This dilemma unclear – both lost in the sphere.

We laughed and talked, beauty laid bare,
No one moved, yet neither could spare.
The love birds dreamt what they couldn't show,
In fate's soft wind, we let it go.

What comes next, we let unfold,
Though dreams dared, none foretold.
This coffee offered – a definite move,
Yet neither knew how one cup could stir more than coffee's groove.

"A Mirror Between Us"

♥

I was surprised to learn of the shared routine,
my hands still trembled–too unsure, too keen.
His steady stance, his voice so warm,
held a calm that could quiet any storm.

Yet my thoughts slipped back to that café's hue,
to whispers and laughter that somehow grew.
The way he looked, the pause, the air–
it all felt heavier than it should dare.

And then he asked–the question I'd guessed,
a truth unspoken now softly confessed.
I smiled, said "yes," as if meant to be,
and something inside bent quietly in me.

♠

A calm disguise I wore that night,
yet her gaze met mine, setting things alight.
Each word I spoke, she caught with ease,
and time stood still between our breaths and tease.

I thought of coffee, her half-smile shy,
the dim-lit table, her curious eyes.
Between each rep, her laughter stayed,
a song my restless thoughts replayed.

At last, I asked—"Shall we keep in touch?"
My tone unsure, my heartbeat rushed.
She nodded once, her silence clear,
and I saved her name—too close, too dear.

Dumbbells clanged, a breath slipped through—
something small had started to move, too.
Not an ending, but a quiet start,
two orbits drifting, inching apart.

No promises made, no big intent,
just simple words, the way glances went.
We laughed, we smiled, but something changed,
the air between us softly rearranged.

The pull grew closer, yet not quite love,
just fate unfolding from above.
One small start, two names exchanged—
and something deeper got quietly arranged.

"Names And Numbers"

♥

Our first late-night talk began so light,
his texts kept flashing through the night.
He spoke of iron, of gyms, of grind,
of brands and goals that ruled his mind.

He liked his words to stay well-framed,
and hated things that stayed unnamed.
I laughed, I teased, I broke his line,
said, "Perfection's dull – mess can shine."

He replied with a grin I could almost hear,
and the night kept pulling us near.
Between his charm and quiet pride,
I saw a warmth I couldn't hide.

♠

Her voice was strange – like fire and free,
no care for rules, no plan, no plea.
She spoke of rain and muddy trails,
of running wild beyond the rails.

She said she liked the world unplanned,
no map, no mold – just open hands.
I liked her laugh, so sharp, so wild,
yet feared her heart would not stay mild.

She said she hates most people's ways,
but loved in silence, not in praise.
I typed, "You're rare," then stared too long –
she sent a meme, turned it to song

Screens glowed soft, the hours flew,
jokes and dreams – both old and new.
Music played – a retro tune,
the kind that melts the heart too soon.

Between each text, a spark would hum,
two restless souls, now beating as one.
He talked of gain, she dreamed of flight,
and both met halfway – that endless night.

Not love yet, but something near,
a warmth too close, a rising fear.
Because even in laughter, fate had sown –
two hearts that would burn, yet not be home.

BARE UNFOLDINGS

"The Quiet Pull"

The iron clanged, my heart keeping pace,
He lifted beside me, calm in his space.
His shoulder brushed mine, a spark I felt,
Ordinary boy, yet my chest began to melt.

I smiled at him, shy but bold,
He laughed at my form, playful and told.
Every rep, every drop of sweat,
Felt like a story I'm not done with yet.

His gaze stayed longer than it should,
Retro music played, soft in the wood.
I wondered if it was a spark or just a sign,
Or is it just the echo of something unclear, yet mine?

♠

She moves with ease, confident, precise,
I watch her energy, playful and nice.
Hands brush the bar, fingers almost collide,
I notice, a spark I try to hide.

She teases my form, challenges my pace,
I laugh along, caught in her trace.
Something about her, different from the rest,
A calm in the chaos, my heart won't rest.

Retro hum wraps around us, soft, discreet,
The gym feels smaller with her heartbeat.
Something stirs in the ordinary we share,
A pull unspoken, hanging in air.

We exchange brushes, smiles, and playful little fights,
Weights and steps turn into shared delights.
Hands almost touch, then drift apart,
Silent sparks weaving through the heart.

Music hums softly, laughter fills the air,
Every moment lingers, subtle and rare.
Accidental touches, teasing words between,
A quiet connection that's felt but unseen.

Even as the gym fades behind us now,
Curiosity and fascination linger somehow.
We leave with a heartbeat not named,
And the mystery of whispers soft, untamed.

· Flickers On The Feed ·

♠

She shares her world, tidy and bright,
Books and lights, small smiles in sight.
A spark of intrigue, simple, true,
Her quiet essence pulls me through.

Her world feels far, untouched, apart,
Yet it whispers softly to my heart.
I stay cautious, curious, aware,
Drawn in by her presence, subtle and rare.

Her posts catch me, gentle and small,
Common place moments that still enthrall.
A quiet rhythm, simple and profound,
Her silent voice, a pulse I've found.

He shows his world, bright and alive,
Friends, workouts, brands that thrive.
Curious, careful, I scroll and see,
Shadows and sparks that tempt me

His eyes in photos, laughter in frame,
A quiet devotion I cannot name.
Our worlds contrast–mine lone, his loud,
Yet something soft breaks through the crowd.

Neither of us perfect, I know it well,
A gentle tug, a cautious spell.
I let a little in, hearts near but shy,
Small sparks linger as screens pass by.

Hearts pause, fingers hover, screens glow,
Curiosity and quiet purpose start to show.
No touch yet, just glances we send,
A slow, lingering digital dance that won't end.

Small likes and comments, subtle and sweet,
Moments between worlds where shadows meet.
Our lives feel apart, yet somehow aligned,
A gentle connection, quiet and kind.

The call ends, the picture remains,
A mix of curiosity, caution, and chains.
A spark is let fly, careful, not fast,
Silent and mysterious, a feeling to last.

"A Walk Through Stillness"

♠

She stood near the doorway, brushing off the sweat,
and I finally said, "It's warm today—maybe a walk instead?"
Her eyes met mine, half amused, half unsure,
but her soft "Sure," felt like something pure.

I took her to the barren garden I often visit alone,
a place where the wind hums and the silence has its own
tone.
She walked beside me, fast and fearless,
and I struggled to match her quiet boldness.

She spoke of chaos, of books and art,
of ruining plans just for fun, a rebellion of heart.
I smiled at her words, half lost in her charm,
wondering how something wild could still feel calm.

♥

He asked me for a walk – I almost said no,
but curiosity made my feet follow slow.
The garden was barren, yet strangely alive,
green leaves whispering as we arrived.

The air was still, though birds would call,
and his quiet presence seemed to fill it all.
He talked less, but his voice was deep,
each word felt like something I'd keep.

He told me of gym, of brands he adored,
how he found peace in things others ignored.
He looked composed, but his eyes gave chase –
a calm man hiding a restless space.

Two shadows moved beneath the quiet moon,
the night breathing softly, a wordless tune.
Laughter fell light, like rain in disguise,
and time stood still under silver skies.

The garden lay still, half-living, half-known,
a silence between us quietly grown.
Maybe it was peace, maybe a start,
a slow-told secret neither could chart.

Moments lingered, soft and low,
something returning we didn't yet know.
A hush, a pull, the calm before,
a mystery repeating—becoming once more.

Between Words & Wind

♠

We spoke again after days apart,
small talks grew softer, close to heart.
The gym still echoed her gentle tone,
but now her texts felt like home.

She told me how she trusts too slow,
how love's a word she doesn't know.
She laughed at trends this world admires,
said she burns different, not like liars.

I said I get it – I've seen worse,
betrayal cuts deep, it's a curse.
I joked about cars, about the race,
while she read the storm behind my face.

His name blinked late, the screen went bright,
a casual "hey" that stretched all night.
He spoke like someone twice his age,
a calm within a reckless cage.

He said he's tough, he plays with risk,
that rules for him don't really stick.
He talked of luxury, fast and fierce,
but something hollow ran beneath the gears.

And yet I stayed – too drawn, too near,
his wrongs became the words I'd hear.
I told myself it's just a phase,
but I was lost in his unreal gaze.

Messages flew like wind through glass,
hours slipped too quick to pass.
Each word built bridges thin and wide,
where truth and danger walked side by side.

Maybe it was fate, maybe a spell,
a spark too strange to name or tell.
But between the laughs, the charm, the play,
a quiet warning began to sway.

Not love, not yet – but something near,
a pull that felt too strong, too clear.
And in that night of screens and sighs,
the wind began to whisper lies.

"Shared Things"

♠

She posts a picture, a meme, a brief joke,
Her world so joyful, bright, and bespoke.
Her likes and shares have a rhythm I see,
A subtle pull that surprises me.

Her style, her humor, the light in her eyes,
Every small post feels like a prize.
I sense a quiet curiosity growing within,
A spark I try not to fully let in.

We love the same music, reels, and trends,
Common threads that the universe sends.
I wonder how ordinary yet unique she seems,
A gentle pull between reality and dreams.

He sends a meme, a reel, a song I enjoy,
His style feels honest, playful, and coy.
I notice his quirks, the cadence he keeps,
A pull I can't name, but quietly seeps.

Curiosity draws me, yet I don't always stay,
Sometimes I hide, sometimes I drift away.
I silently bide a gentle distance,
Balancing intrigue with cautious persistence.

I let moments come, then softly break,
Not every message keeps me awake.
Still, his presence lingers, subtle and near,
Something quietly stirring, delicate and clear.

♦

Snapshots, memes, reels shared with delight,
Giggles and quick looks in the soft internet light.
Little moments that outlast passing days,
Where our worlds converge in quiet ways.

Jokes, music, inside jokes we send,
A rhythm that seems to naturally blend.
Every message, every post, sparks a glow,
A soft warmth breaking through the shadow.

We don't speak our feelings out loud,
Yet each exchange leaves a mark, subtle but proud.
Curiosity and fascination quietly swirl,
A gentle prelude to what's soon to unfurl.

THREADS OF GOLD

Echoes Of The Past

I told her once, not proud but true,
how love once failed, how trust withdrew.
My best friend stole the girl I kept,
and every promise quietly slept.

Since then, faces blurred, names fade,
girls around felt bought, not made.
Their talk of luxury, gold, and fame,
none could set my heart aflame.

But she – she said she'd rather ride,
on an old Activa, right beside.
Not car or cash, just wind and time,
that line of hers rewrote my rhyme.

♥

He spoke of pasts like breaking glass,
his voice too calm for scars that vast.
Said pain had turned his heart to steel,
yet in his words, I saw him feel.

I told myself to stay away,
but some strange force made me stay.
Not his charm or his careless tone,
but something raw I'd never known.

He wasn't like the rest, I swore,
he spoke of loss but wanted more.
And though I feared this pull, this spin,
it felt like fate had reeled me in.

♦

Two voices met between the ache,
a comfort neither planned to make.
His wounds were loud, her calm replied,
both found warmth where pain could hide.

Maybe this was healing's start,
or just two cracks aligned in part.
Whatever it was, it softly grew –
a haunting calm we both called *new.*

Neither named it, nor wished to define,
But something shifted between his and hers, in line.
Perhaps it was healing, or maybe a mistake–
A mystery they didn't yet understand, repeating.

•Walls I Didn't Mean To Break•

♥

I told him once, love isn't kind,
it bruises heart, and clouds the mind.
That trust for me was long misplaced,
a wound the years could not erase.

He listened quiet, not to reply,
but something softened in his eye.
And suddenly my practiced walls,
felt thin, like paper before it falls.

I said I'm tough, that I don't chase,
but his calm pulled me into space.
I should've left before I knew –
but I was falling, slow and true.

♠

She spoke of storms she had survived,
how dreams can fade though hearts have tried.
Her words were fragile, soft, and bare,
and somehow, I was breathing there.

I told her pain makes strength anew,
that broken hearts still beat in hue.
But deep inside, a selfish spark,
loved the way she lit my dark.

She called it healing; I called it fate,
though I knew it came too late.
For in her trust, I saw my gain –
a warmth I'd crave, not keep, again.

Under the silence of night, two hearts spoke low,
Sharing pieces they'd never let show.
New warmth met the ache of old scars,
And quiet carried what words could not far.

Her guard was falling, slow and slight,
His charm too smooth beneath the light.
What they called healing, time would test,
For comfort often hides unrest.

They didn't know what fate would send,
What parts would break, what parts would bend.
A secret stirred, unseen, unknown –
A mystery repeating, yet their own.

·The Words on Screen·

♠

The screen glowed soft in the dark of night,
typing and erasing, chasing what felt right.
My heart was loud, my hands unsure,
three words hovered – raw, impure.

I hit send before I could refrain,
"I love you." My pulse, insane.
No voice, no touch, just text and fear,
but the silence after felt too clear.

Maybe I should've waited, slow,
but feelings grow where secrets go.
Her typing dots began to blink,
and time itself forgot to think.

The phone lit up, my breath held tight,
three words stared back – soft, yet bright.
I didn't plan for this tonight,
but my heart felt oddly light.

He said it first – I didn't guess,
but somewhere in me said "yes."
Not out loud, but through the air,
a quiet warmth, too much to bear.

I typed and stopped – erased, then wrote,
each word like waves that barely float.
"I feel the same," was all I sent,
not knowing what the message meant.

♦

Two blue ticks, two souls aligned,
across the distance, hearts entwined.
No music played, no world around,
just echoes soft – no louder sound.

Screens became their only space,
a digital touch, a coded grace.
And love began where light was dim,
a spark that bloomed from quiet whim.

They didn't know what would unfold,
that warmth can turn from soft to cold.
And in that glow, the mystery grew,
a loop repeating – old, yet new.

Beginnings in Bloom

♥

His "good morning" *pinged before sunrise,*
a start of days wrapped in surprise.
Between the small talk and the laughter shared,
I almost forgot to be scared.

He'd say, "you look tired, don't skip meals,"
and I'd smile at care that suddenly feels.
How strange that comfort can bloom so fast,
in the soil of things that never last.

I told him once, "maybe we're too soon,"
he laughed —"then let's make time our tune."
It wasn't love yet, but close enough,
a tenderness disguised as tough.

Each text she sent, a quiet delight,
turning dull days into softer nights.
I'd scroll back just to read again,
her words like calm after the rain.

I joked, I teased, but underneath,
my heart forgot how to breathe.
She was the calm I never earned,
the peace for which the restless yearned.

When she said, *"I don't trust easily,"*
I smiled – *"then let me prove steadily."*
Maybe I was falling, maybe too deep,
but her name kept echoing in my sleep.

♦

The world outside stayed loud and gray,
yet their chats made the noise decay.
A shared screen, a spark unseen,
made distance fade to something serene.

No vows exchanged, no heavy claim,
just simple joy without a name.
But love, disguised as laughter and text,
was already learning what comes next.

And far below, where silence grows,
a familiar pull, the mystery rose.
It whispered softly, "wait and see," –
for what feels new has history.

Threads of Midnight

♠

She texted, "I love the smell of rain."
I rolled my eyes – but typed, "Same."
Funny how the words I'd never mean,
started to feel too soft, too clean.

She said she'd rather ride on two,
than in my car that's built brand-new.
And yet that line – so small, so plain –
stayed with me more than champagne.

Her talks of love, of peace, of home,
pulled me where I'd never roam.
And though I laughed, I couldn't lie –
I'd trade my pride to see her smile.

♥

His voice, that blend of calm and wild,
made the world around turn soft and mild.
He said, ***"You dream too much, too deep,"***
I smiled, ***"That's how my heart will keep."***

He liked his cars, his rush, his brand,
yet held my dreams inside his hand.
A man of metal, but eyes of rain,
how strange he made me love again.

He said, ***"You're not like girls I know."***
I said, ***"That's why I move too slow."***
Our chats grew quiet, deep, and true –
two minds rebelling, yet aligned too.

Between the texts, the night stood still,
words wandered where hearts would spill.
Rain tapped softly, screens aglow,
as laughter hummed through all they'd know.

Dreams were spoken, secrets shared,
two souls confessed how much they cared.
He spoke of cars, she spoke of skies,
their worlds met under quiet sighs.

Each message stitched a thread so thin,
that neither knew where it had been.
A mystery whispered soft, unseen,
growing between each word and screen.

•The change Which Came•

♥

He said hope was a myth, that miracles don't stay,
Life was meant to be hard, to carve your own way.
Yet somehow, through chats in midnight's hue,
I saw his edges soften – something new.

I told him I love the rain and children's cheer,
That vows mean promise, not a burden to fear.
He laughed at first, said forever's a word too deep,
But I saw his silence – the thoughts he'd keep.

He spoke of scars and lessons he'd earned,
Of bridges burnt and dreams overturned.
Still, every text, every call we made,
Felt like hope he unknowingly displayed.

♠

Miracles don't happen – that's what I knew,
Life hits hard; you fight your way through.
Yet she spoke of rain like it healed her soul,
And I found myself losing control.

She said love is steady, like vows in bloom,
That marriage isn't a cage, but a living room.
Her laughter painted warmth in my dark routine,
Her chaos calm – something serene.

I never liked kids, nor skies that cried,
But I liked how she made me feel inside.
If change had a name, it'd sound like hers,
A comfort I never knew was hers to confer.

Two hearts once apart began to align,
Through words, through dreams, between each line.
Her faith in forever, his disbelief in the same,
Met somewhere soft – neither lost, nor tame.

Between laughter and silence, a bridge was spun,
Where endings dissolved, and hopes begun.
The world outside kept rushing fast,
But time stood still – their change would last.

And in the calm of the moon's soft view,
Something stirred – the mystery grew.
What they called "change," fate already knew,
A lesson in love, old yet new.

In the Arms of the Night

♠

The moonlight dripped softly outside the café, silver spilling on the floor,
I drowned in her eyes, in the way her laughter poured.
Every word she spoke felt like rain falling slow,
And something inside me whispered —*don't ever let her go.*

Her soft chuckles tangled with the night air's sweet grace,
Her vanilla scent wrapped the edges of this place.
I gave in, pulled her waist, tugged her tight to stay,
Pressed her close, where heartbeat met the fray.

Her curves, her warmth, the rhythm of her breath,
My chin on her head, silence soft as death.
I could feel the world shrink, the noise turn still,
In that single embrace, I lost my will.

She fit in my arms like time fit the night,
Soft chest against mine, her body feather light.
I wanted to live there, beneath that soft moon's dome,
Because for the first time... someone felt like home.

♥

I was lost in our chatter, in laughter spilling free,
He listened so closely, like I was poetry.
Then suddenly, without warning, it came through –
His hands on my waist, pulling me to something true.

The world blurred out, the café dimmed to a glow,
His cologne wrapped around like a tide's slow flow.
His manly hands carved their way around me tight,
And the moon above held witness to the night.

His heartbeat thundered against my racing chest,
My breath fell short, but my soul felt blessed.
He stood tall – like a storm I wanted to meet,
And I melted softly in that steady heartbeat.

His hold said things no words ever could,
And for a moment I stayed where I never thought I would.
I felt so small, yet so alive in his hold,
A warmth too precious, too fierce to be told.

The café lights dimmed, the world fell small,
Two hearts collided like they'd known it all.
No grand music, no fireworks in the sky,
Just silence and breath, where love learns to lie.

His arms spoke louder than lips could dare,
Her warmth met his in the cool night air.
Between ribs and whispers, the world aligned,
The line between strangers quietly resigned.

And somewhere in the quiet, something began to thread,
A mystery born where two souls were led.
They didn't know yet where this story would go,
But the night had a plan they'd slowly come to know.

Under the Moonlight

♠

We sat under moonlight, beneath whispering trees,
The night hummed softly, carried by the breeze.
I drowned in her gaze, sweet jasmine and night,
Every inch of her presence pulling me right.

Her pink lips glimmered, like honey in the dark,
My heartbeat roared, like a flint to a spark.
I tucked a stray strand, lifting her jaw with care,
Our breaths tangled softly, hanging midair.

For a moment, the world held its breath too,
An unspoken question lingered between two.
Her eyes were oceans, I wanted to dive,
Her lips were a spell keeping me alive.

I whispered, "May I?" – soft, like wind in sleep,
She nodded gently, as the world fell deep.
Her lips under mine, soft, delicate, sweet,
And time itself knelt at our feet.

♥

His eyes traced me, a gaze slow and sure,
I saw his breath waver, the night felt pure.
He tucked a strand behind my ear with grace,
And I froze under the weight of his face.

His brown eyes burned, his sharp jaw defined,
His pout of pink pulled me in, entwined.
Under the moonlight, he seemed unreal,
Like a storybook man too vivid to feel.

"May I?" he asked, his voice steady, low,
I nodded before my mind could say no.
His hands cupped my jaw, his thumb brushed my skin,
And the stars above swore the night would begin.

Our lips met softly, no fight, no chase,
Just rhythm and warmth in a perfect place.
His pulse in my chest, our breaths aligned,
That kiss wrote a story – wordlessly defined.

♦

The night paused as their worlds intertwined,
Every second a spell, every breath entwined.
No fireworks, no grand parade to see,
Just two hearts whispering, "it's meant to be."

The breeze slowed down, the sky leaned near,
The world grew quiet so they could hear.
A kiss not rushed, but carved slow in air,
Two souls tangled in something rare.

They didn't know where this road would bend,
But a mystery softly began to descend.
The moon kept their secret, the night held its breath,
Not love just yet – but a promise beneath.

"His Name My Smile"

♠

Late calls turned to quiet nights,
Her laughter softened city lights.
She spoke of dreams she'd one day own,
Of building riches all alone.

I told her, "You'll get there, just wait and see,"
But deep inside, I hoped she'd stay with me.
She talked of freedom, I talked of pride,
Two hearts in sync but worlds collide.

One night I said, "You're all I claim,
If I could, I'd give you my name."
Her silence stretched, a half smile grew,
And something old in me felt new.

She smiled, said softly, "You talk too deep,"
And blushed in ways my chest would keep.
I held her close, no fear, no shame,
Not knowing what storm this love would name.

♥

His voice through phone lines felt like home,
A warmth I'd never known.
He'd talk of dreams, of cars and fame,
And I'd just smile, say, "We're not the same."

I told him how I'd earn my name,
Stand tall, make my own flame.
He'd say, "You're fire, you'll light the way,"
And my walls fell more each day.

He'd text me first, send songs by night,
Talk about fate and stars in sight.
Each word was soft, each glance sincere,
Too perfect, too close, too dear.

Still, I felt a whisper deep in my chest,
A voice that said, "Don't call this best."
But his care was warm, his words were right,
And I stayed wrapped in that soft night.

Two voices echoed, night to dawn,
Bound by dreams they built upon.
He saw her fire, she saw his calm,
They thought love's chaos could bring them balm.

Each chat stitched comfort into days,
Each call a thread in gentle maze.
They laughed at fears, the past they fled,
Not knowing where those threads had led.

It looked like peace, it looked like grace,
Like fate had smiled upon their space.
But in the calm, a shadow crept –
A mystery whispered, soft and kept.

The Quiet Cracks

♠

I brought her ice cream, cold and sweet,
Her tired eyes, my calm retreat.
Said, "Rest, my girl, you've done enough,"
I liked her soft when life got tough.

We'd talk for hours, from dusk to dawn,
About her goals, the road she's on.
I'd tease her dreams, say, "Stay with me,"
She'd smile, "No love can cage the free."

Her strength impressed, her will divine,
But power's thrill still clouded mine.
I wanted her near, not far to roam,
Even care can start to feel like home.

Still, I'd watch her breathe and drift,
Her name in my chest, a holy gift.
Yet something cold began to bloom,
A quiet pride that darkened the room.

He came with care, with ice cream too,
Said, "Rest today, I've got you."
His love was steady, firm, and kind,
Yet something strange hid in his mind.

We'd talk on call, we'd laugh, we'd tease,
He'd say, "You're mine," with practiced ease.
And though my heart would softly melt,
A warning in his gaze was felt.

He'd ask, "Where were you?" when I'd be late,
I brushed it off – said, "It's fate."
He smiled again, but the tone was low,
A love that started soft, began to show.

Still, he'd hold me when I cried,
Promise forever, never hide.
And I, too lost in the dream we spun,
Ignored the cracks that had begun.

It looked like love, so pure, so real,
Wrapped in comfort no wound could heal.
They built a world of perfect hue,
Believing care could hide what's true.

He gave, she glowed, the story stayed,
In hearts too young, illusions played.
A bond so soft, yet bound so tight,
A warmth that dimmed the warning light.

But somewhere deep, fate wrote again,
That comfort often turns to pain.
And what began in silver rain,
Would end repeating – yet not the same.

THE STILLNESS BETWEEN THE HEARTS

The Call

♥

His name flashed across my phone that night,
A trembling call, a quiet fright.
He said, "I'm fine, just bruised my knee,"
Yet my heart raced faster than it should be.

I wanted to run, to see him breathe,
To hold his pain if it meant relief.
My strict home walls couldn't confine,
The pull I felt wasn't simply mine.

He whispered, "Don't worry, I'll be okay,"
But worry had already found its way.
That call stayed replaying, like fate's sign,
As if my calm had crossed a line.

♠

I didn't mean to scare her that night,
But hearing her voice made things feel right.
The accident was small, yet her care was vast,
Like she'd been waiting for a reason to ask.

She said my name like it meant the world,
And something in my chest quietly unfurled.
Her worry was warmth I didn't deserve,
Still, I stayed, feeding off her nerve.

When she hung up, silence burned slow,
I liked knowing she couldn't let go.
Some part of me wanted her near,
More than I wanted the pain to disappear.

The night hummed low, our hearts aligned,
Through wires, comfort intertwined.
An accident minor, yet hearts were stirred,
Something shifted–without a word.

The night stitched us close in hush and care,
a quiet promise floated in the air.
No thunder, no vow, just soft concern,
a lesson love forgot to learn.

The stars blinked twice before fading to grey,
something gentle began to stray.
We didn't hear the echo's plea–
even calm nights hide what's yet to be.

The Visit

♥

I went to see him the very next day,
My heart knew what my mind couldn't say.
His hand in bandage, smile still bright,
I froze between guilt and delight.

He laughed, "It's just a scratch, don't fuss,"
But I still held his wrist, too much for us.
The scent of antiseptic mixed with his cologne,
That small room felt like our own.

I sat beside him, words running late,
He said, "You care too much–it's fate."
I smiled and brushed his messy hair,
Pretending not to drown right there.

♠

She came in pink, with fear in her tone,
And turned that dull room into home.
She scolded me softly, "Drive slow next time,"
Her voice was rhythm, her care divine.

I liked that she came despite her walls,
That her softness answered my calls.
Her fingers lingered longer than they should,
And I realized–her love felt good.

When she left, she looked once more,
My soul followed her out the door.
I knew that this wasn't small or mild,
She looked at me like I was worth the trial.

Two hearts sat close, one bruised, one torn,
From fear and longing, something was born.
The air grew thick, the silence warm,
Even pain began to take new form.

The room breathed warmth, not quite our own,
a stillness heavy, yet softly sewn.
Care felt pure, but shadows stayed,
in tender light, our doubts decayed.

A smile, a sigh, the hush of rain,
we swore we'd never feel this pain.
Yet under comfort's velvet gleam,
truth slept silent, dressed in dream.

Candlelight Confessions

♥

The night was quiet, screens aglow,
Messages deeper than we'd known.
He said, "You make me believe again,"
And my chest pulsed under my skin.

He told me of dreams, of scars, of pain,
How loyalty was all he'd gained.
I wanted to tell him I'd stay through storms,
That I'd learn to love in different forms.

When his "I love you" came through the screen,
I smiled–half scared, half serene.
I typed, "I think I might too,"
And watched the night turn something new.

♠

Her typing dots blinked like sparks of fate,
My hands trembled; I couldn't wait.
When she replied, my heart took flight,
Her words turned darkness into light.

No loud promises, no sudden vow,
Just quiet truth–I'd found her somehow.
She was chaos, warmth, and peace in one,
My midnight moon, my rising sun.

I wanted her near, I wanted her real,
To touch her hand, to make her feel.
I swore then, I wouldn't let go,
Though something inside whispered–"Don't show."

Love arrived without a sound,
In typed words where hearts were found.
Two souls confessed under faint screens' hue,
And fate began its dance anew.

Bodies spoke where words grew shy,
our breaths entwined beneath the sigh.
We thought the stillness meant we'd won–
but love was learning how to run.

Moonlight held what hearts concealed,
half of us spoke, the rest unsealed.
Something sweet began to ache–
a perfect calm before the quake.

The Ride

He said, "Let's escape, just for tonight,"
And I agreed beneath city lights.
The wind tangled through my hair,
His laughter hummed in the open air.

We rode past crowds, past noise and fear,
His hands on the throttle, the world unclear.
I leaned behind, my arms around,
For once, I felt my heart unbound.

I whispered, "Don't let go," mid-race,
He smiled, warmth brushing my face.
It wasn't danger–it was something deep,
A promise neither of us could keep.

♠

She held me tight while the roads bent wide,
And I swore the stars leaned close that night.
Her voice echoed between the breeze,
It sounded like a prayer, set to tease.

I felt her laughter on my back,
The kind of joy I'd always lacked.
For once, speed didn't mean escape,
It meant holding her, heart to shape.

She said, "You're safe with me tonight,"
And I believed her under that moonlight.
Little did she know—her words, they tied,
A restless man, to calm inside.

Two shadows chased the road ahead,
Unspoken words were all they said.
The wind was wild, the world was small,
And they didn't know they'd risk it all.

Two truths met softly, none too loud,
we built our peace without a crowd.
Hope was fragile, almost kind–
but fear still lingered, undefined.

We dreamed aloud of days ahead,
not hearing what the silence said.
The stars were listening, sharp and clear,
they knew what we refused to hear.

The Room of Quiet

♥

He called me home, his tone unsure,
"I'm alone, and the night's a blur."
I went, though rules held me tight,
My heart already lost that fight.

The room was dim, the couch was near,
He said, "You're safe, I'm right here."
Our laughter broke the weight of air,
And warmth grew wild everywhere.

I rested beside him, calm yet near,
His fingers brushed away my fear.
It wasn't wrong–it just felt known,
Like finding a piece I'd never owned.

♠

She came in light, in scent and hue,
Her eyes like dawn, her words so true.
We talked of dreams, of paths, of pain,
Till silence kissed us once again.

Her head fell softly on my chest,
Her breath aligned with my unrest.
I didn't speak, I only stayed,
The world outside quietly decayed.

When she slept, I whispered low,
"You've no idea how far I'd go."
It wasn't love–it was something more,
A fire both gentle and unsure.

In quiet dark, two souls aligned,
Through warmth that wasn't yet defined.
No vows, no plans, no claim, no name–
Just two hearts learning they felt the same.

Our lips wrote stories without sound,
the world fell off, no solid ground.
We thought we found where love begins–
not seeing cracks beneath our skins.

When dawn returned, our hearts still burned,
but something vital never turned.
In warmth so pure, we lost the clue–
that every nearness alters truth.

The Stillness Between Heartbeats

♥

He kissed me slow, the world stood still,
As if love bowed to a stronger will.
His breath was warmth, his eyes a plea,
A moment carved in memory.

His fingers traced my face to lips,
A pull so soft, my heartbeat slips.
He held me close, his breath so near,
The world fell quiet – only him to hear.

Our lips aligned, a hush, a sigh,
Time stood still beneath the sky.
A gentle hum, a spark, a light,
Two souls adrift through silent night.

His touch was gentle, his voice unsure,
But my trust in him felt pure.
For once, the chaos inside me slept,
As silence softly, sweetly wept.

♠

Her lips were soft, like prayer or art,
And I kissed her deep to claim her heart.
Not to own, but to make her stay,
To bind her warmth in my own way.

I couldn't get enough – I knew I won't,
Her warmth a truth I'd never confront.
Our breaths entwined, the world stood still,
Desire soft, yet fierce in will.

Her eyes met mine, no words, no guise,
A silent fire beneath those skies.
As my lips found hers, both lost in bliss,
The stars looked down on our fervent kiss.

She whispered, "I trust you," under breath,
A vow that echoed close to death.
Her innocence was too divine,
I almost wished it wasn't mine.

Between heartbeats, they became one,
Under the gaze of a setting sun.
It felt like forever, quiet and wide–
But love was changing, deep inside.

We slept in faith the night was ours,
counting mercy instead of scars.
But morning eyes can change their hue–
even devotion shifts its view.

We didn't see the thread grow thin,
how comfort dulls what burns within.
The mystery stayed–soft, unseen–
love felt endless, but never had been.

BURNT ASHES OF WHAT ONCE WAS

•Distancing In Familiar Eyes•

♥

It's been a year, and I've stopped showing up at the gym,
He says the new one's closer – still, his tone sounds dim.
The phone buzzes less, reels stay unsent,
It's love, I tell myself, maybe just content.

He laughs less now, calls feel timed,
I reread our chats – the "forever" lines.
When I asked, "Busy?", he just said "You know me."
But his words carried a distance I didn't see.

Once we breathed in sync, like one single art,
Now we talk like strangers learning to start.
And though he says he's tired, needs space –
Something inside me feels out of place.

♠

Routine became noise, messages blurred,
I told her "work's heavy", but said no word.
She teased, "Maybe your other girlfriend?", and smiled,
I replied, "You never know, bbg," half-wild.

I saw her face fall – quiet, unsure,
Her silence lingered, pure and mature.
I didn't mean harm, I just wanted peace,
But the truth is, her presence makes my rest cease.

She's warmth, I'm frost; we both knew the signs,
Yet I stayed between the guilt and lines.
Not a villain, just a man turning cold,
In her love, I've lost the hold.

The screens still glow, but the words are few,
Ghosts of laughter drift through the blue.
Two hearts still beating, but far apart,
Something's slipping between pulse and heart.

He says "maybe later," she says "it's fine,"
They both lie soft between each line.
The world stands still, their stories thin,
This is where the distance begins.

The Date That Didn't Heal

He said, "Let's meet tonight – I'll make it right."
And I, naive, dressed in white.
The café lights shimmered, my heart knew hope,
Maybe we'd heal, maybe we'd cope.

He smiled faintly, but eyes stayed away,
His hands on the phone – mind miles astray.
I spoke of plans, he just hummed low,
Love shouldn't ache, but it does, you know.

We drove back home – the road was still,
He said, "You've changed," I said, "Maybe you will."
He kissed my cheek, not my lips this time,
And that was how love lost its rhyme.

♠

I took her out because she asked for more,
But I couldn't recall what I felt before.
Her laughter echoed, once my cure,
Now it stung – too pure, too sure.

She said, "*Remember how we met that day?*"
I nodded, though my mind was far away.
A part of me wanted to pull her near,
Another part whispered, "*You don't belong here.*"

Her eyes searched mine – I turned aside,
Truth and guilt, both I tried to hide.
Sometimes you break what you swore to protect,
Not from hate, but quiet neglect.

♦

They met where love once bloomed in grace,
Now silence filled that sacred space.
The same table, the same old view,
But the warmth was gone – they both knew.

No anger spoke, no tear was shed,
Just quiet ghosts of what was said.
Love didn't end in thunder or cries,
It just slipped away in tired goodbyes.

And somewhere deep, fate softly sighed –
"You came back to the circle where it all died."

When We Were Still Us

♥

We fought and fixed it every time,
his voice would melt in whispered rhyme.
He said, "You're the calm in all my mess,"
and I believed his every guess.

He'd text, I miss your stupid face,
and I'd reply, I'm on my way.
Little fights, but love would win,
like waves that crash, then pull us in.

Now looking back, the peace feels far,
like chasing light from fallen stars.
We laughed too loud, we stayed too late,
I thought that love could change our fate.

She'd pout when I forgot her calls,
then laugh again – no grudges at all.
Her silence spoke, I knew her tone,
even anger made me feel at home.

I'd say, "You overthink too much,"
she'd roll her eyes, escape my clutch.
Yet every fight would end in peace,
a soft "I'm sorry," love's release.

Now even texts don't sound the same,
we talk in circles, play the game.
The love that bloomed now fades too fast,
a dream too perfect, built to last.

We had our storms, we had our sun,
we broke apart, then merged as one.
Each tear we shed, each scar we kissed,
was proof of how much we'd be missed.

But maybe peace was never meant,
for hearts so loud, so permanent.
We tried too hard, we held too tight,
and lost our spark beneath the fight.

The mysteries we once ignored,
returned like lessons, unexplored.
Repeating circles, déjà vu–
as if we'd done this once, or two.

"Arms Around a Fading Sky"

♠

Outside the café, the city slept,
her laughter fell, the distance crept.
I reached for her waist without a plan,
a fleeting warmth, the ghost of a man.

Her scent was jasmine, soft, the same,
but even that now whispered my name.
Her breath on my skin, her voice so near,
I held her tight – to silence my fear.

She fit my arms like she did before,
but love felt tired, not tender anymore.
I thought, *if we end, let this hug stay,*
for once we were right, before we decay.

♥

He pulled me close beneath the light,
his chest against me, steady, right.
I felt the tremor, the silent fight,
the warmth that burned a little too bright.

I smelled his cologne, his heartbeat loud,
we stood unseen by passing crowd.
My lips formed words that never spoke,
he held me tighter, my calm just broke.

It felt like goodbye dressed up as care,
his touch too soft to mean he's there.
I closed my eyes, I didn't cry,
I just let the night be our last try.

♦

Our hearts aligned in fragile peace,
a hug pretending love won't cease.
The moon looked down, the stars leaned low,
as if they'd seen this long ago.

His hands, her breath – the same old tune,
two fading souls beneath one moon.
We held like first, we held like last,
embracing both the now and past.

Maybe this was the karmic bind,
a love once lost, again to find.
Not to hold, not to win–
just to learn what lies within.

"The Kiss That Knew Goodbye"

♠

Her lips were trembling, eyes half-closed,
the air between us quietly froze.
I brushed her hair, she looked away,
I whispered, "We'll be fine someday."

But in that pause, I felt the truth,
our love was old, outgrowing youth.
I kissed her slow, my soul confined,
a taste of what I'd leave behind.

It wasn't passion, it was prayer,
to bless the love we couldn't repair.
Her tears were salt, her lips divine–
a promise fading line by line.

♥

He leaned so close, my pulse betrayed,
his fingers found my jaw, then stayed.
His breath on mine, his words too kind,
but kindness kills when hearts unwind.

His lips met mine, the world went still,
a storm of warmth, a void to fill.
It didn't burn, it didn't thrill,
it only whispered, we always will.

And as we broke, I felt the scar,
not of distance – but who we are.
For this goodbye, too, I knew before,
it echoed from another shore.

The night grew cold, the sky bent low,
our shadows merged, then let us go.
A kiss that promised, yet denied,
love that stayed, yet slowly died.

We met before, we'll meet again,
in dreams, in mirrors, through the pain.
But this lifetime knew its end tonight,
and still, it felt strangely right.

Maybe this loop was never curse,
but love rehearsed across the verse.
To love, to lose, to love again—

a circle soft, a tender chain.

He Called It Space

He used to text at dawn, now his replies crawl through the day,
I see the glow of his phone, he turns it the other way.
"Who's that?" I tease, half-laughing, half-afraid to know,
"You never know, bbg," he says, a mocking echo.

He says he's "busy," that "work's just too much,"
But busy hearts still find the ones they clutch.
The reels stopped, the calls slowed down,
Yet I kept defending him when no one was around.

I tell myself this distance's just a phase,
A storm that passes, a shift in maze.
Still, every night I pray he'll write,
The same old boy from our first moonlight.

♠

I need some quiet; she doesn't understand,
Love's a burden when it gets out of hand.
She wants updates, calls, the same routine,
I just need space to breathe in-between.

She jokes about girls, but the tone cuts deep,
I laugh it off – secrets I keep.
Not that I cheat, just wander around,
A king in a circle who lost his crown.

She's all heart, I'm all fight,
She wants forever, I want tonight.
It's not that I don't love her – I do in my way,
But commitment's a price I can't pay.

◆

The distance grew but we called it "space,"
Two moons orbiting the same place.
Words unspoken still found their trace,
And love turned cold behind the face.

Some nights we laughed, pretending fine,
But fate was drafting a different line.
Every goodbye we didn't say was still a sign –
A mystery repeating, same design.

The Words That Sounded Like Love

♥

He'd say, "You're mine, my calm, my fire,"
and pull me close like worn-out wire.
Those words stitched comfort in my bones,
a melody I called my home.

He said he'd give me all his name,
a promise soft, yet hard to claim.
I carved it deep, as if divine,
believing every "you are mine."

Now I replay those nights in bed,
his whispers still inside my head.
The same ones healing what once tore,
now echo where they live no more.

♠

I told her things I thought were true,
but truth is shaped by time's own hue.
Back then, forever felt so real,
like something words alone could seal.

She looked at me with endless faith,
and I mistook that look for grace.
But people change, the days grow long,
and love forgets its favorite song.

Still, part of me won't let it fade,
the peace we built, the plans we made.
If loops exist, if fate's still kind,
perhaps I'll meet her one more time.

Our words became our gentle cage,
sweet lines that aged before their age.
Each "mine" we said was half a lie,
yet true enough to justify.

We held our faith like fragile glass,
pretending cracks would never last.
And in that stillness, we both knew,
love can be kind, and cruel too.

The mystery circled, soft, unseen—
was it his voice, or one I'd dreamed?
As if in lives we'd lived before,
he'd said those words and left once more.

The Exit Wound

♥

He said, "Don't overthink, it's not that deep,"
But I'd stayed awake through nights of no sleep.
Love shouldn't feel like chasing proof,
Yet I kept defending the bullet as truth.

His "busy" hours turned to vanishing days,
His words grew sharp in subtle ways.
Every time I reached, he'd pull away,
Still I waited, thinking he'd stay.

Then I saw it – the smirk, the lies,
He loved the power in my teary eyes.
He liked the way I still forgave,
A puppet dancing, love his stage.

♠

I knew she'd stay, no matter the storm,
Her heart too gentle, her faith too warm.
Her care wrapped me like endless light,
A comfort I craved but couldn't make right.

She was too soft for the walls I built,
Too steady for my fleeting guilt.
Control was a thrill I couldn't release,
I mistook her love for borrowed peace.

I never meant forever, just a while,
A passing spark, a borrowed smile.
When she cried, I turned away,
Some truths are crueler than what we say.

The night was quiet, the truth too loud,
Two souls breaking under a cloud.
She searched for love; he searched for pride,
The wound was love's – the cut was wide.

Maybe he'll tell himself he cared,
Maybe she'll wish she never dared.
But deep down both hearts knew,
He was never hers – he only passed through.

The stars above blinked cold and dim,
She learned pain has no mercy in him.
It wasn't fate, or loop, or bend –
Just a red flag dressed as a friend.

"Echoes Of The Same Goodbye"

♥

I no longer count the months or years,
Since the boy I loved walked out the door.
"You are my forever, my name, my home," he swore –
But forever was brief, and left me sore.

His words, "Don't cry, baby, you'll never feel pain,"
Still whisper through the midnight rain.
But I've learned what it means to break
By the hands that once helped me heal again.

I gave him everything – my light, my soul,
Even the shadows I'd promised to control.
He filled the void, then tore it wide,
Leaving love's unfinished side inside.

Perhaps it's the same old ending, in another heart –
History repeating, worlds apart.
You were the echo, he was the sound,

THE AFTERLIGHT

The Memory That Wasn't Mine

I had seen this heartbreak once before –
not here, not now, but in a life unspoken.
His eyes, his smile, his leaving too –
a pattern the universe had never broken.

Each goodbye felt strangely rehearsed,
each ache knew exactly where to land.
It wasn't the first time my heart had cracked –
just another echo slipping through my hand.

Maybe I was chosen to remember,
to finish what I'd left undone before.
And though the pain felt freshly carved,
my soul whispered, "We've been here before."

Love Was Just the Mirror

He wasn't the love – he was the mirror,
the gleam that showed my own disguise.
Every word he said, I'd said in silence,
every touch he gave, I'd already idealized.

He mirrored my ache, my hunger for care,
the part of me I had never fed.
I wasn't loving him – I was loving
the version of myself I thought was dead.

And when he left, he didn't take much –
only the illusion, the shadow, the art.
I looked in the mirror and saw his eyes,
but this time, they were just my heart.

The Afterlight

I'm no longer sixteen and waiting,
no longer asking "why me, why this pain."
Love came once dressed as a boy,
and left as a quiet, cleansing rain.

I still walk by that café sometimes,
the one where forever began to fade.
Now I smile – not in sorrow, but knowing
some storms come to teach, not to stay.

Maybe he was never mine to keep,
just the lesson I was meant to learn.
Because endings too, when faced with grace,
are a form of love that never returns.

***∞"I wasn't remembering him.
I was remembering me —
before I forgot who I was."***

In Retrospect

As you've stayed with me till the final line of this book, let me tell you what lay between them – the parts that never made it to the page.

I was sixteen, maybe seventeen, when love first found me – or rather, when I mistook longing for love.

The girl who never looked up from her world of poems and paintings suddenly did.

And for the first time, I wasn't just the poet; I was the poem.

People often saw me as an extrovert – smiling, social, the one who lit up every room – but behind every laughter there was an echo. A hollow.

I loved company but was never truly seen.

There were strict walls at home, a bond with my sibling that dimmed with time, and parents who loved me, but never really heard me.

The world called it a perfect teenage life.

But how could perfection exist in nights spent with a restless mind and tearless eyes?

It began in a gym – two strangers, quiet glances, a few words that felt like a spark.

He was charming in a way that made the world slow down.

Chats turned into conversations that ran past midnight.

He approached first – confident, composed, the kind of presence that feels like a promise.
His voice felt familiar, his gaze almost ancient.
It wasn't meeting someone new; it was remembering someone lost.
And that's how it began – glances that became words,
words that turned into hours,
hours that turned into love.

He told me, *"I love you,"* and I believed him. I believed him, someone few months quite older than me. I know a little naïve.

Because when you're sixteen and lonely, even lies can feel like lullabies.

He checked up on me – my studies, my meals, my silences.

He said he loved my mind, my chaos, and one day, "You'll have my name."

At sixteen, I believed in forever.

Maybe because I'd never felt so seen before.

For once, the void inside me was filled — or at least, I thought it was.

He said, *"You'll never be hurt again,"* and I thought I was safe.

He kissed me under a dim café light — gentle, assuring,

as if forever lived in that single breath.

We laughed about small things, shared secrets, dreams, fears.

He made promises that painted futures we were too young to live.

There were drives, coffee dates, warm hugs, words that felt like home.

Every time his hand met mine, the world felt steady again.

He said, "You're my forever."
And I, naive but sincere, built my world around that sentence.

But slowly, forever began to fade.

He changed gyms, stopped sending reels, his texts grew shorter.

The calls that once felt endless turned into polite exchanges.

When I teased, "Maybe you've got another girl," he laughed – a little too carelessly – and said, "You never know, bbg."

Something inside me cracked, but I ignored it.

That's what love makes you do – ignore the noise for the memory of peace.

He said he was busy, stressed, tired.

I told myself love required patience, and I gave him mine.

But love that demands silence is rarely love at all.

He avoided my eyes, changed topics when I asked to see his phone. He mocked my worries, saying, "You think too much."

He didn't show up one evening – no call, no message, no reason.

And I realized I'd fallen for the kind of man who liked being adored more than he liked me.

Red flags weren't always red – sometimes they were disguised as effort.

When I cried, he'd hold me close, whisper, "Don't cry, baby, you'll never feel pain."

But love shouldn't have to come with reassurances that sound like warnings.

He wanted control, not connection.

He liked being the reason behind my smile, not the person keeping it safe.

He wasn't cruel – just careless with what I handed him so gently.

When I met him one last time,his hug didn't feel like safety – it felt like a goodbye he wouldn't say aloud. And then came the final kiss –deep, trembling, cruelly gentle.

It didn't taste like love; it tasted like endings.

When he left, there was no closure, no explanation.

Just silence loud enough to break me.

I replayed every word, every promise.

"Was it boredom? Another girl? Or had he simply gotten used to me?"

None of the answers mattered, yet all of them hurt.

Because when someone becomes your comfort, their absence feels like losing a piece of yourself.

Healing wasn't pretty. It wasn't overnight.

It came in waves – anger, doubts, grief, acceptance.

I realized I wasn't healing from him, but from what I allowed.

From believing love meant sacrifice.

From giving my all to someone who only wanted pieces.

He mirrored my love, not his own.

And maybe that's why it felt so familiar —like a story I'd already lived, in another time, another version of me.

And sometimes, the hardest part of growing up is *realizing that the same person who healed your wounds was sent only to reopen them — so you'd learn to close them yourself.*

So yes, I was sixteen,but I carried a soul far older than my age —one that loved fiercely, broke quietly, and wrote it all down to survive.

Because healing isn't pretty. It's acceptance.

It's saying, ***Yes, I was betrayed. Yes, I was heartbroken. Yes, I needed love.***

It's knowing the trauma doesn't leave — but neither do you

I'm older now, though the memory still stings.

Sometimes I wonder if he remembers me — the girl with stars in her eyes and a heart too pure for the kind of love he could offer.

Maybe he doesn't. Maybe that's the point.

Because this wasn't a tragedy, it was a lesson —that some people come not to stay, but to awaken.

And if you've ever felt the same — empty, yearning, betrayed —know this:

You are not weak for feeling deeply.

You are not foolish for loving freely.

You are human, and that's what makes your story worth telling.

This isn't a fairytale.

It's my story — and it still echoes in me every day.

And as you close this book, know that the silence you feel screams in my chest every single day.